JERUSA

GW00992339

THE CHUᴋᴄн
OF THE
HOLY SEPULCHRE

JERUSALEM

THE CHURCH
OF THE
HOLY SEPULCHRE

An Introduction & Guide

STEPHEN W. NEED

Best Wishes,

Stephen Need

cartaJerusalem

First published in 2016 by
CARTA Jerusalem

Editor: Lorraine Kessel

Photographs:
All photographs are by Stephen W. Need, except for:
Looking up at the inside of the Rotunda, on page 73 is by Samuel Magal
Frontispiece: The entrance plaza to the Church of the Holy Sepulchre,
is by Samuel Magal.

Drawings and Plans:
© Carta, Jerusalem

All quotations from the Bible are from the New Revised Standard Version.

- Great care has been taken to ensure that the information in this guide is accurate at the time of publication. However, Carta cannot be responsible for any outcome that may stem from errors, omissions or inaccurate information.
- Sudden changes may occur. You are advised to inquire from the competent authorities about visiting times, security arrangements and updates ahead of your planned visit
- The publishers shall be grateful for any changes, errors or inaccuracies brought to our attention. All such will be incorporated in the next edition.

Carta Jerusalem, Ltd.
11 Rivka Street, POB 2500
Jerusalem 9102401, Israel

E-mail: carta@carta.co.il
Website: carta-jerusalem.com

ISBN: 978-965-220-880-4

Printed in Israel

TABLE OF CONTENTS

Preface 7

Part One: 8

Introduction 8

The New Testament Background 12

Death by Crucifixion 16

Burial in a Tomb 20

When Did Jesus Die? 24

Jerusalem City Walls 26

Constantine's Church 31

The Intervening Years 39

The Crusader Church 43

Christian Groups in the Church 47

(1) Greek Orthodox 47

(2) Armenian Orthodox 48

(3) Roman Catholic or Latin, and Franciscan 49

(4) Coptic Orthodox 51

(5) Ethiopian Orthodox 53

(6) Syrian Orthodox 54

Part Two: 56

**Guide to the Church of the
Holy Sepulchre** .56

Approaching the Church 56

Outside the Church 59

Inside the Church .61

Calvary 63

The Rotunda and Tomb 66

Chapels Around the Church 73

And Finally... 79

**Church of the Holy Sepulchre:
A Rough Chronology** 80

Bibliography and Further Reading 84

for Canon John and Kirsten Peterson

PREFACE

About twenty years ago now I began taking students of St. George's College, Jerusalem to the Church of the Holy Sepulchre in the Old City of Jerusalem. This Introduction and Guide is the outcome of work done during that period and is intended to provide visitors and pilgrims with a basic understanding of the church and its background.

The Church of the Holy Sepulchre stands over the places where tradition says Jesus was crucified, buried, and rose from the dead. It has attracted pilgrims for 1600 years and is used today by six different Christian denominations. Wherever you come from, your time in Jerusalem will be incomplete without a visit to this church—it is the central shrine of Christendom.

Part One of the book can be read at home or in your hotel room before visiting the church. It is an introduction to some of the many different aspects of the history and development of the site. What do the gospels say about the events commemorated here? How were people crucified and buried at the time of Jesus? How many churches have there been on this site? And why is the present-day church inside the city wall when surely Jesus was crucified outside the wall?

Part Two is a guide to the church itself and is for use inside the building. Taking you on a simple walking tour, it points out basic features such as Calvary, the tomb of Jesus, various chapels, and many other items of interest.

The book does not attempt to identify every part of the church's history or to comment on everything inside the building. But by the time you have read and used it you should be familiar with some of the most important aspects of this unique and holy place.

I hope you enjoy your visit to Jerusalem's famous Church of the Holy Sepulchre.

Stephen W. Need
Essex
England
July 2016

PART ONE:

INTRODUCTION

The Old City of Jerusalem stands 2,500 feet above sea level in the Judean desert. Its complex and fascinating history stretches back millennia. Ruled for centuries by infamous kings, emperors, and caliphs, it is sacred to Jews, Christians, and Muslims alike. Its unique position in the world's three monotheistic faiths gives it a powerful religious mystique and magnetism.

For Christians, the focal point of the Old City is the Church of the Holy Sepulchre (or "Church of the Resurrection" as it is also called) in the Christian Quarter. This famous building marks the traditional sites of the death, burial, and resurrection of Jesus. The entrance is

Main dome and east end of the Church of the Holy Sepulchre

concealed in a maze of winding streets and disappearing alleyways. Local Arab markets swell out on every side with clothes vendors, bric-a-brac stalls, coffee shops, and restaurants all touting for trade. But the church is well worth finding. For many pilgrims and tourists it is one of the most important stops on the Jerusalem itinerary, telling its own powerful story and breathing its own unique spirituality.

Originally built in the fourth century by the first Christian emperor, Constantine the Great, the church was destroyed in the eleventh century by the so-called "mad" Caliph Hakim of Egypt and then rebuilt by the Crusaders in the twelfth century. Repeatedly damaged down through the ages by attacking armies, earthquakes, and fires, it nearly collapsed early in the last century through shear neglect. Today the church is in better shape than it has been for years, due to negotiation, renovation, and repair.

Much can be learned by spending time in the Church of the Holy Sepulchre. Some visitors are surprised by what they find inside. The exotic liturgies of the Orthodox Churches often shock Western Christians, the hustle and bustle of pilgrims usually distracts those who seek a quiet corner in which to pray, and the whole edifice seems to bear little relation to the "green hill far away" of childhood Sunday school classes and hymns. For others, however, the ancient stones of the church speak of history and faith, its down-to-earth atmosphere tells of humility and incarnation, and in the midst of human confusion and mess, some claim, God's calming presence is almost tangible.

Whatever your reaction to the Church of the Holy Sepulchre you will only appreciate it fully by understanding something of its long, complex history and development, beginning with Jesus himself and stretching down to the present day. This introduction will give you a basic overview of that history and development.

Crusader façade of the Church of the Holy Sepulchre

The cross above the central dome of the Church of the Holy Sepulchre

THE NEW TESTAMENT BACKGROUND

There is no doubt that the death and resurrection of Jesus are central to the writers of the New Testament. St. Paul, the earliest, is clear that these events are the basis of Christian faith. In his first letter to the Corinthians he says, "For I decided to know nothing among you except Jesus Christ, and him crucified" (2:2). His big chapter on the resurrection (15:1–58) in the same letter shows how important the risen Christ was to him. In 15:3–11, Paul gives his account of Jesus' death, burial, and resurrection although he provides hardly any historical detail. He is clear in his other writings too that the cross and resurrection of Jesus are central. In Romans he sees the death of Jesus as the centerpiece of God's act of salvation for humanity. Referring to the cross, he says that God put Jesus forward "as a sacrifice of atonement by his blood" (3:25). And in his letter to the Philippians, Paul is clear that Jesus' death on a cross and his subsequent exaltation are the center of salvation for humankind:

"And being found in human form, he humbled himself and became obedient to the point of death—even death on a cross. Therefore God also highly exalted him" (2:8–9).

Other New Testament writers have a similar emphasis. The author of the Epistle to the Hebrews makes the death of Jesus on the cross the center of his entire theology when he refers to it as the "once for all" sacrifice that brings to an end all the sacrifices of ancient Judaism (10:1–10). And in the Book of Revelation, Jesus' death on the cross is symbolized by the sacrifice of the lamb whose blood is shed for the salvation of the world (5:1–14).

Better known to most Christians are the accounts of the crucifixion and resurrection of Jesus in the New Testament gospels of Matthew, Mark, Luke, and John. The earliest, Mark, focuses almost entirely on the cross and its importance in the lives of the disciples. The others include resurrection appearance stories. In Mark's account of the passion of Jesus, the key events are laid out as follows: the Palm Sunday entry into Jerusalem, often known as the Triumphal Entry (11:1–11); the so-called Cleansing of the Temple (11:15–19); the Last Supper (14:12–26); the betrayal of Jesus in Gethsemane (14.32–50); the trial before the High Priest (14:53–72); the trial before Pontius

Jesus carrying his cross as portrayed in the Franciscan chapel

Pilate (15:1–15); the crucifixion (15:16–39); the burial (15:40–47); and the empty tomb (16:1–8). The other gospels, especially Matthew and Luke, follow Mark but there are significant differences of detail. For example, Jesus' dying words differ in the four gospels: Mark and Matthew have, "My God, my God, why have you forsaken me?" (Mark 15:34; Matt 27:46); Luke has "Father, into your hands I commend my spirit" (23:46); while John has his dramatic "It is finished" (19:30). The differences here reflect the individual evangelist's theological outlook and emphasis.

Following Jesus' death in these narratives, as the Sabbath day

Domes and towers of the Church of the Holy Sepulchre

dawns, his body is laid in a tomb. On the third day, the tomb is found empty. Again, the gospel accounts differ. In Mark, some women come to the tomb early in order to anoint Jesus' body for burial. They find that the stone to the tomb has been rolled away and that the body is gone. A young man tells them that Jesus is not there; he is risen and has gone to Galilee (16:1–8). This account is now considered by most scholars to be the original ending of Mark's gospel; the resurrection appearances (16:9–20) were added later. Matthew has the same basic empty tomb story but now an earthquake occurs and an angel appears, giving the message of Jesus' resurrection and saying that he has gone to Galilee (28:1–10).

There is then an appearance of Jesus on a mountain in Galilee where he commands the disciples to go and make disciples of all nations (28:16–20). In Luke the empty tomb story is much the same as Mark, but now the risen Jesus appears to the two disciples on the road to Emmaus (24:13–35) and again in Jerusalem (24:36–49). Finally, in John's gospel the account is quite different from the others: the beloved disciple outruns Peter to the tomb (20:1–10); and Jesus' burial cloths are specifically mentioned (20:5–7). The dramatic resurrection appearances are now to Mary Magdalene who thinks Jesus is the gardener (20:11–18); to the disciples including the "doubting" Thomas who is invited to put his hand into Jesus' wound (20:19–29); and again to the disciples on the shore of the Sea of Galilee (21:1–14).

The differences among the gospel accounts of the last days of Jesus' life are striking but they all say that he died on a cross, was buried in a tomb, and rose from the dead. Quite a lot is now known about what his crucifixion and burial might have looked like.

Death by crucifixion: one of many possible reconstructions of a crucified man

DEATH BY CRUCIFIXION

Most Christians today have little concept of what crucifixion in first-century Judea was like. Few of the crosses in our churches portray how horrific it really was. Mel Gibson's film *The Passion of the Christ* emphasizes Christ's sufferings but doesn't adequately portray the realities of crucifixion.

There is no doubt that Jesus died on a Roman cross. In addition to the four New Testament gospels there are other sources that confirm this. Some of the apocryphal gospels, for example the Gospel of Peter, tell of Jesus' death on a cross. The first-century Jewish historian Flavius Josephus refers to it, as does the later Jewish text known as the Mishnah (ca. 200 CE). The Roman writer Tacitus (first century) mentions Jesus' execution. The Syrian writer Mar bar Serapion (first century) also refers to Jesus' death. And the rhetorician Lucian of Samosata (second century) refers to the crucified man of Palestine. So what do we know about crucifixion as a form of capital punishment at the time of Jesus?

First, crucifixion in the ancient world was more widespread than is often thought. It may have originated among the Persians but it soon spread widely among the Indians, Assyrians, and Carthaginians, among others, as well as among Greeks, Jews, and Romans. It was known just as much in the west as in the east. It was widespread because it helped enforce power, authority, and social control, especially of slaves. For those who were condemned to death it was a vicious form of punishment. Violent criminals, anyone that had

Jesus crucified as shown on Greek Calvary

betrayed the state, committed murder, or inspired rebellion could die by crucifixion. Although practiced widely, it was the Roman form of capital punishment *par excellence* . There were different procedures: most criminals died on the cross itself, while others were killed first and their bodies then displayed on the cross. The Jewish practice of hanging the body on a tree (Deut 21:21–23) is basically of this second type. The crosses, upon which bodies, dead or alive, were displayed, could be of any shape. The person might hang upright, upside down, or in some other position. In the Greek and Roman worlds, thousands of people could be crucified at a single time.

Contrary to popular imagination and artistic portrayal, when it came to the crucifixion itself the criminal usually carried only the cross bar (Latin: *patibulum*) to the place of crucifixion. The upright beam

Statue of St. Helena in the Chapel of the Finding of the Cross

(Latin: *stipes*) was usually waiting in place at the chosen location. The criminal's outstretched arms were then nailed or bound to the cross upon arrival. The nails would have gone through the wrists or arms rather than the palms of the hands to prevent the flesh from tearing. The criminal would most likely have died from suffocation, asphyxiation, or heart attack. The loss of blood would have been enormous and the pain unbearable. This is why a small seat or rest (Latin: *sedile*) would have been supplied under the buttocks so that the person could ease himself up and take a breath. This could help prolong life for some time but would also prolong pain. The criminal might take days to die but would usually be dead within hours. Certain drinks like hyssop and vinegar might be given to help deaden the pain, as in the case of Jesus (Mark 15:36). Some details of the practice of crucifixion in the ancient world have been

revealed by the discovery at Giv'at ha-Mivtar in Jerusalem in 1968 of the bones of a crucified man. In this case the heel bones were found still bolted together with a nail.

Death by crucifixion had several purposes. The ultimate form of humiliation, it was, of course, a strong deterrent. Onlookers would see the detestable manner in which the criminal was dying and feel a degree of satisfaction and revenge as they perceived justice being done. The process also provided a certain amount of entertainment. In this respect it is comparable to the other popular form of execution in the Roman Empire: being thrown to wild beasts. Most crucifixions would have been of criminals from the lower classes and when the person finally died he would not be buried. Bodies would be left on the crosses to be eaten by birds and wild animals. When the body had finally been eaten, the bones would be taken away and disposed of. If the body was taken down soon after death it would in most cases be thrown into a common grave. For those who could afford burial, however, there were several options.

BURIAL IN A TOMB

The gospels give limited details about Jesus' burial but what we are told fits well with what we know about tombs and burial in Judea during the period of the second temple (536 BCE–70 CE). The recent discovery of the so-called "Jesus family tomb" in Talpiot near Jerusalem has ignited wide interest in tombs at the time of Jesus. The Talpiot tomb is almost certainly not Jesus' family tomb but the question of the type of tomb he had is important. How were Jewish people buried at the time of Jesus? Unless the body was left on the cross to decay, there were basically four possibilities. First, most people would be buried in a common grave. They would not have been able to afford any other burial. They would have been thrown unanointed into a mass grave.

Ossuaries from the so-called Jesus family tomb, and other ossuaries from the period of the second temple, found in Jerusalem
Author: Tamarah
Via Wikimedia Commons

Rolling Stone tomb at the excavations of the Sisters of Nazareth

Second, if they were wealthy enough they could have been buried in an "oven (Hebrew: *koch;* plural *kochim*) tomb" sometimes known as a "rolling stone" tomb. The "rolling stone" tomb was so named because it had a stone that rolled to and fro in a groove across the doorway. Inside this type of tomb was a chamber in which the body would be prepared for burial, usually by anointing. It would then be slid into a body-length niche cut into the rock with an opening in the shape of a semicircular oven. If this was a family tomb, there would be several of these areas into which the bodies of other family members could be placed. After about a year to eighteen months when the body had decomposed, the family came and scraped the bones out of the tomb area and placed them in a stone box called an ossuary. This was then taken away to another location and given a secondary burial with other ossuaries. This method of burial was the most popular during the Second Temple and Byzantine periods in Judea.

Third, again requiring wealth, was a tomb with an *arcosolium* shelf (Latin: *arcus*, "arch" and *solium*, "throne"). In this, the body was anointed and then placed onto a shelf in the wall of a burial area similar to those in the catacombs in Rome. As with the *koch* tomb, after the body had disintegrated the family would come and take the bones off the shelf and put them into an ossuary and take them away to another location for secondary burial.

Arcosolium shelf as seen in the archaeological site of excavated Roman Ostia, Italy
Author: Camelia.boban
Via Wikimedia Commons

The fourth type of burial at the time of Jesus was not so common but is more familiar to westerners. This was burial under the soil in a simple trench grave. We know that this form of burial was used in the Second Temple period because the graves of over 1100 bodies buried in this style quite close to the surface were found at Qumran where the Dead Sea Scrolls were discovered from 1947 onwards. These may have been bodies of the Essene community that most scholars have associated with Qumran. Some have speculated whether the Essene belief in resurrection influenced their manner of burial.

Thus, four styles of burial were known in the Second Temple period in Judea: mass graves; *kochim* or rolling stone tombs; *arcosolium* shelves; and trench graves. In which way was Jesus buried?

Some commentators distrust the gospel accounts of Jesus' burial claiming that because he was not wealthy he would have been buried in a mass grave or that his body would have been left on the cross to decay. However, all four New Testament gospels tell us that a wealthy man called Joseph of Arimathea provided Jesus with a new tomb. Mark calls him "a respected member of the council" (15:43) who took Jesus' body and laid it in "a tomb that had been hewn out of the rock" (15:46). This already suggests that Joseph might have been wealthy. Matthew then adds, "a rich man from Arimathea, named Joseph" (27:57). Luke says that Joseph of Arimathea laid Jesus' body in "a rock-hewn tomb where no one had ever been laid" (23:53). John's gospel also says that Joseph laid Jesus' body in "a new tomb in which no one had ever been laid" (19:41). The gospels say that because it was the time of preparation for the Sabbath, the body of Jesus was left in the tomb until someone could return to anoint it (Mark 15:42–47). Mark says that Joseph of Arimathea then "rolled a stone against the door of the tomb" (15:46).

Several important things emerge from the gospel accounts. First, that Jesus was buried in a tomb by a wealthy man and not thrown into a pauper's grave. Second, the tomb was of the rolling stone

Two 'kochim' tombs in the Syrian chapel

Candles burning inside the church

or *koch* type. Third, because the Sabbath was coming, the body was left (presumably) in the chamber of the tomb, so that when the women came back after the Sabbath it could be anointed and then slid into one of the oven-shaped niches in the rock. It is clear from the gospel accounts that this is what the women were on their way back to the tomb to do on that Sunday morning (Mark 16:1). But when they arrived, the body was gone. It is thus also clear that Jesus' body, though dead, never underwent full anointing and burial.

The gospel accounts of Jesus' burial make perfect sense if the context was a rock-cut, rolling stone, or *koch* tomb typical of the Second Temple period in Judea. Two *kochim* tombs of exactly this type can be found today in the Syrian chapel in the Church of the Holy Sepulchre just behind the so-called tomb of Christ.

WHEN DID JESUS DIE?

Most scholars today believe that Jesus was crucified sometime between 29–33 CE but they cannot be absolutely certain when. It is notoriously difficult to establish dates in the ancient world because people worked with different calendars and the sources available are ambiguous and conflicting. We know that Jesus died when Pontius Pilate was Roman Prefect in Judea (Matt 27:2; John 18:28–29; Acts 3:13) and when Joseph Caiaphas was High Priest in Jerusalem (Matt 26:3, 57; John 11:49; 18:13, 24). Pontius Pilate was Prefect from

26–36 and Caiaphas was High Priest from 18–36. These two men had important and powerful positions in Roman and Jewish society and their times in office set the parameters for the possible dates of Jesus' crucifixion. We also know that Jesus died on a Friday at the time of the Feast of Passover, the most sacred feast of the Jews. It was celebrated on the 14th of the Jewish month Nisan, which is the equivalent to our March–April.

Beyond this it is difficult to be exact about when Jesus died. There is a discrepancy between the Synoptic Gospels (Mathew, Mark, and Luke) and John concerning the date. In the Synoptics, the Last Supper is a Passover meal and Jesus dies the following day (Friday, 15th Nisan). But in John's Gospel he dies at the time of the slaughter of the lambs in preparation for the Passover meal that evening (Friday, 14th Nisan). This means that in John the Last Supper is not a Passover meal. It looks as though the author has changed the timing of the crucifixion so that Jesus dies at the same time as the Passover lambs. This fits in with his theology of Jesus as the Lamb of God (John 1:29). In the light of this, the synoptic chronology has usually been seen as more historically reliable.

The Last Supper
Engraving by William James Linton (1812-1897) from a
19th century Bible,
Colored by Carta, Jerusalem

The next important thing to work out is in which year 15th Nisan fell on a Friday. This is a complex matter and other factors, such as the date of the beheading of John the Baptist and the length of Jesus' ministry, also influence the calculation. Some scholars have concluded that Jesus died early in the possible period and others later but most conclude that he was crucified in the middle years of Pontius Pilate's reign, probably in early April around 30 CE.

JERUSALEM CITY WALLS

The next important element in understanding the story of the Church of the Holy Sepulchre concerns the various walls that surrounded Jerusalem at the time of Jesus and afterwards. Contemporary pilgrims to Jerusalem are often confused to find the church that stands over Calvary and the tomb deep inside the city walls. They are familiar with the nineteenth-century hymn written by Mrs. Cecil Frances Alexander (1818–1895), "There is a green hill far away, Without a city wall...." For a start, there is no "green hill" and the church stands

The tomb of Christ

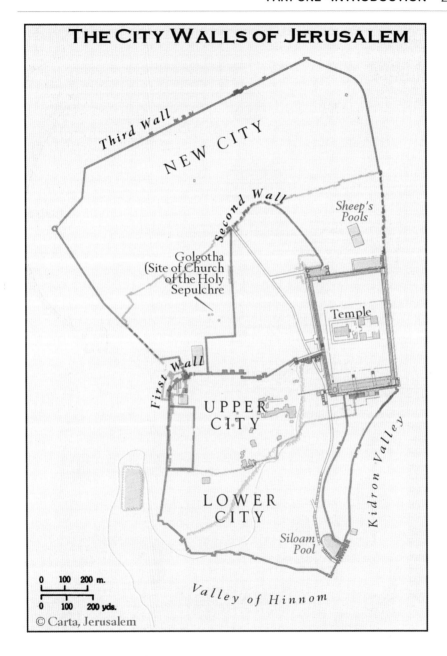

Map showing the development of the 'three walls' of Jerusalem.
Note how the third wall brings Golgotha inside the city.
Carta, Jerusalem

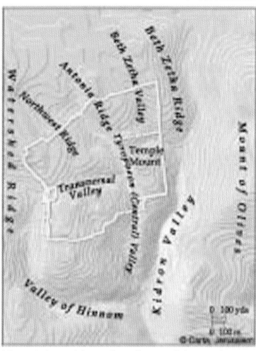

Mountains, ridges & valleys of Jerusalem

inside the city wall. Of course, "without a city wall" means "outside a city wall" as distinct from "inside" or "within a city wall." The hymn romanticizes the location of Jesus' death but it is important to appreciate that during his day the place where the church now stands was indeed outside the city wall of Jerusalem. The present-day wall was built by the great Muslim ruler Suleiman the Magnificent in the sixteenth century and was not there at the time of Jesus. But the story of the wall at the time of Jesus is important for understanding how Calvary came to be inside the wall and how a church was eventually built over the place of his crucifixion and resurrection.

Jerusalem is built on a ridge surrounded by three important valleys: the Kidron (John 18:1), the Gehenna (or Hinnom) and the Tyropoean (or Cheesemakers). The area is riddled with ridges and valleys, including the Mount of Olives and Mount Scopus on the eastern side. The city was surrounded by different walls at different times in its history. By the time of Jesus, it had already had several walls since it had grown and developed up the hill from the original City of David to the much bigger city known to Jesus.

The first-century Jewish historian Flavius Josephus refers to three walls of the city of Jerusalem, but he is only counting the ones starting from the century before him. Josephus's "first wall" was a wall that ran round from the area of the Pool of Siloam to the Temple Mount. Golgotha, where Jesus was crucified, was well outside this. When Herod the Great (king of the Jews: 37–4 BCE) extended the temple area he put in a "second wall" enlarging the city considerably but still excluding the area of Golgotha. At the time of Jesus the area of Golgotha was a quarry where stone was produced for building. It had become a place of crucifixion and burial, and was therefore outside the city wall as demanded by the Jewish Law and authorities on grounds of health. There is a great deal of scholarly debate about the exact route of this second wall but most scholars believe that the place of crucifixion was indeed just outside rather than just inside the wall. The discovery of two Second Temple period *kochim* tombs inside the Church of the Holy Sepulchre indicates that the area was indeed originally outside the city wall rather than inside. Golgotha or Calvary, the place where Jesus was crucified and buried, was thus "outside the city wall." The first Christians would have visited the site to remember the events of Jesus' death and resurrection.

The next step in the development of the city wall is of major importance. In 44 CE Herod Agrippa, Herod the Great's grandson, expanded the city limits considerably, almost doubling the size. He put in a new wall, known to Josephus as the "third wall," which brought Golgotha or Calvary inside the city. The place where Jesus was crucified "outside the city wall" (of Herod the Great) was now brought "inside the city wall" (of Herod Agrippa). This wall was not finished during Agrippa's reign and was only completed in the years immediately preceding the Jewish War when the city was being

Arch leading to the Parvis

prepared against possible Roman invasion, which became a reality during the war in 66–73 CE.

After the Jewish War, when the city and temple were destroyed by the Romans under Titus and the Tenth Legion, the street plan of Jerusalem changed. The Roman city built by the Emperor Hadrian (117–138 CE) was renamed Aelia Capitolina and a typical Roman street plan was used. In Roman cities there were usually two main streets: the north-south *Cardo*, and the east-west *Decumanus*. Sections of the *Cardo* of Roman Jerusalem have been found in the Jewish Quarter of the Old City. It is not altogether clear where the *Decumanus* was. According to Eusebius of Ceasarea, Bishop of Caesarea in the fourth century and now known as the "father of church history," Hadrian also leveled out the area of Golgotha filling it in with concrete and setting up a shrine to the goddess Aphrodite

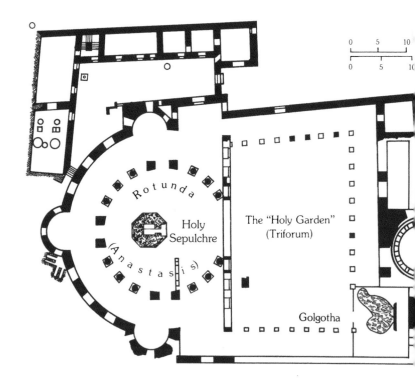

*The Byzantine Church of the Holy
Sepulchre built by Constantine the Great.*

(Venus). It is not clear what Hadrian's intentions were but he may have been hoping to obliterate the site of Jesus' crucifixion and tomb.

It was on the site of Hadrian's temple and of Calvary and the tomb that the Emperor Constantine the Great and his famous mother Helena built a grand basilica in the fourth century. This spectacular building stood off the main *cardo* (Latin: *cardo maximus*) inside the city wall of Byzantine Jerusalem.

CONSTANTINE'S CHURCH

The first church on the traditional sites of Jesus' crucifixion, burial, and resurrection was built by the Emperor Constantine the Great. Constantine was the first Christian emperor and his place in the history of Christianity is pivotal. He had already risen to be emperor

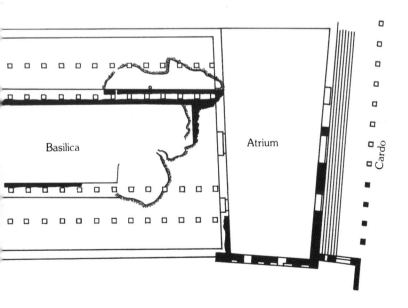

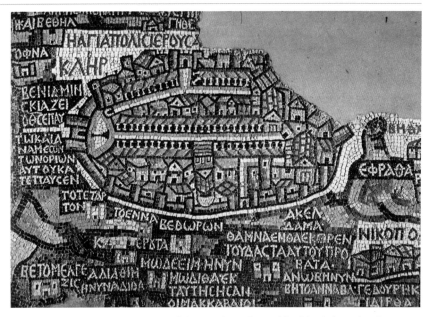

Sixth-century mosaic map of Jerusalem found in Madaba, Jordan
Source: W:en:Image:Madaba_map.jpg
Author: W:en:User:Brandmeister; Via Wikimedia Commons

of the Western Roman Empire when in 312 he defeated his rival Maxentius at the famous battle of the Milvian Bridge near Rome. According to Eusebius of Caesarea and others, Constantine had a vision around the time of the battle in which he saw the *chi rho* (the first two letters of Christ's name in Greek) in the shape of a cross in the sky and was converted to Christianity. Subsequent Christian tradition maintained that Christ led Constantine to victory. Constantine then agreed with Licinius, emperor in the east, that the Christians would be tolerated. Until that time Christianity had been an illegal religion. Later in 324 Constantine defeated Licinius and became sole emperor. At this point he inherited the controversy raging in the church over the teaching of Arius in Alexandria. In 325 CE, Constantine called the Council of Nicaea to address this and other matters. Macarius, bishop of Jerusalem from about 313 until his death around 334, was present.

It was at this council, according to Eusebius, that Macarius and Constantine agreed to build a church in Jerusalem over the site of Jesus' death, burial, and resurrection. The emperor also built churches in Bethlehem, on the Mount of Olives, and in Mamre, south of Hebron. Constantine's mother Helena was involved in some of these projects. The main source of knowledge for the Church of the Holy Sepulchre is Eusebius's *Life of Constantine,* which tells how the area built over by Hadrian was uncovered and the tomb of Christ brought to light. Instead of obliterating the tomb, Hadrian's temple had effectively marked it for posterity. There can be no proof that the tomb of Jesus was the one found by Constantine's workmen, but Eusebius is confident that the real one had been found. Constantine himself was prepared to spend a great deal of money on building a grandiose basilica that would mark the place. Eusebius tells the story of how Constantine's workmen discovered the tomb:

Reconstruction of the Edicule, after an ampulla, c. 500

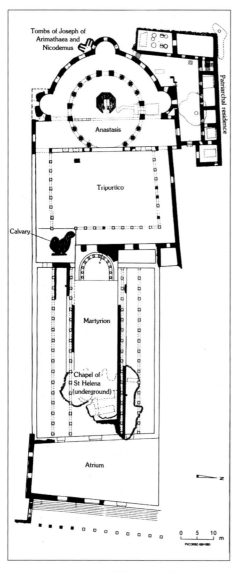

Constantinian buildings at the Holy Sepulchre, after Fr. Corbo. Remains appear in black.

"...as soon as the original surface of the ground, beneath the covering of earth, appeared, immediately, and contrary to all expectation, the venerable and hallowed monument of our Savior's resurrection was discovered."
(Life of Constantine 3:28)

From Eusebius's account, from the writings of subsequent Christians who saw the building, and from recent archaeological excavations in the area, it is possible to get a fairly comprehensive picture of what the church was like. The mosaic map, dating from the sixth century and discovered in the nineteenth century in the Orthodox Church of St. George in Madaba south of Amman, Jordan depicts the Church of the Holy Sepulchre standing proudly just off the main cardo in Byzantine Jerusalem. This is one of the most striking sources for our knowledge of the church and it gives a sense of its size and significance. The cardo ran north-south through the city roughly along the line of today's Khan-ez-Zeit Street, the main street stretching from the Damascus Gate to the Dung Gate.

The church was oriented in a westerly direction and focused on the tomb of Christ. There were four basic parts to the building, which was about 130 by 60 meters:

(1) steps from the street led up to an outdoor atrium that was open to the sky. This was a general porch area that introduced the main building; (2) three doors led into the main body of the church, known as the Martyrion (witness). This church was a witness to the saving death and resurrection of Jesus. The Martyrion consisted of five aisles with a central nave and four rows of columns. It was covered with marble panels and polished stone. The roof was covered with lead on the outside, and the inside was, "finished with sculptured panel work … like a vast sea, over the whole church; and being overlaid throughout with the purest gold, caused the entire building to glitter as it were with rays of light." (*Life of Constantine* 3:36)

The nave led up to a high altar situated in an apse at the west end; doors then led out into (3) an open-air courtyard known as the Triportico. Three sides of a square had columns and the floor

was of highly polished stone. High up on the southeast corner of this square was the rock of Calvary where the "true cross" upon which it was believed Christ had died was set; (4) on the fourth side of the courtyard a door led into the domed tomb area known as the Rotunda or Anastasis.

The Rotunda housed the tomb of Christ, which as far as we know was set inside a polygonal chamber. A number of later sources, including flasks from Monza and Bobbio in Italy, a model in Narbonne, France, and the mosaic in the church of Santa Pudenziana in Rome, indicate that this *edicule* or "little house" was the shrine building in which the tomb

Inner entrance to the tomb of Christ

was set. It stood under a dome with twelve columns "embellished with silver bowls of great size" (*Life of Constantine* 3:38) and was itself highly decorated. According to Eusebius, Constantine spared no expense and the entire church was richly decorated with marble, stone, and gold hangings. He had written to Bishop Macarius that, "it is fitting that the most marvelous place in the world should be worthily decorated" (*Life of Constantine* 3:31). There were also other buildings that surrounded the church, namely accommodation for clergy and pilgrims. The architects were Zenobius and Eustathius and the church was dedicated on September 14th, 335 with the Emperor Constantine present.

The building of the Church of the Holy Sepulchre in Jerusalem and the Church of the Nativity in Bethlehem inaugurated a golden age of Christian pilgrimage to the Holy Land. Pilgrims from around the world began to flock to visit the places where Jesus was born, had died, and was raised from the dead. One of the earliest pilgrims came from Bordeaux, France in 333. He refers to Constantine having built a church on the site where the Lord was crucified and rose from the dead. Later, the pilgrim nun Egeria (sometimes known as Etheria and probably from Spain) tells of her experiences of the Holy Week liturgies in the Church of the

Armenian mosaic of the crucifixion

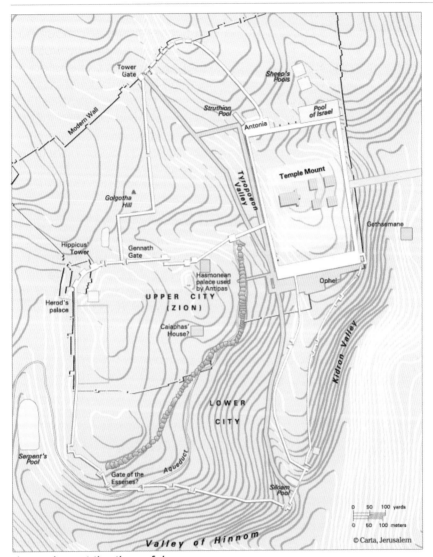

Jerusalem at the time of Jesus

Holy Sepulchre in Jerusalem during her stay between 381 and 384. Much of what she describes fits in with what is known about the church from the sources already mentioned. Toward the middle of the fourth century (ca. 348–350), Cyril, Patriarch of Jerusalem, indicates some features of the church in his *Catechetical Lectures* regarding the baptism of new Christians. It was clearly a striking edifice, which dominated Christian life in the city.

Constantine's basilica was a major development on the skyline of Jerusalem but it was not to last forever. The parts that survive today can be seen in the back of Zalatimo's sweet shop just off Khan-ez-Zeit Street, in the Russian excavations of Alexander Nevsky close to the church, and at one or two points inside the church itself.

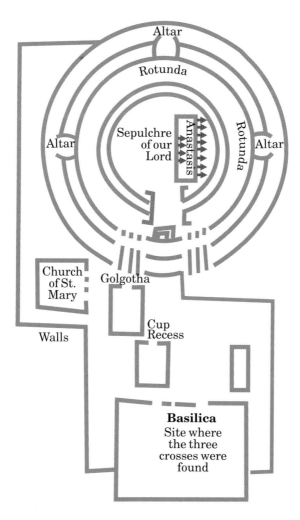

Church of the Holy Sepulchre
and Adjoining Buildings
(After Arculf & Adomnan)

THE INTERVENING YEARS

In 614 the Persian King Chosroes II (also known as Khusrau II) sacked Jerusalem and took away the relic of the "true cross" that had been in Constantine's church (it was later returned). Hundreds of people were massacred and many churches were badly damaged including the Church of the Holy Sepulchre. Structurally, however,

Entrance to the Church of the Holy Sepulchre;
from a postcard titled: Jerusalem (Palestine) 1921.

Constantine's building survived pretty well intact and Chosroes later gave permission for renovation under the guidance of Modestus, abbot of St. Theodosius's Monastery near Bethlehem. Soon after this the new religion of Islam spread rapidly across the region and Jerusalem was taken by Muslims in 638. However, the church was again spared destruction. The Patriarch of Jerusalem at the time, the eloquent Sophronius (remembered today for his sermons and poetry) surrendered to the Muslim leader, Caliph Omar, whom he invited to pray in the church. Omar declined on the grounds that the church would be taken into Muslim hands if he did so. In this way, the church avoided damage and takeover.

According to the English monk the Venerable Bede (ca. 673–735), a pilgrim called Arculf from France visited the Holy Land during this period and stayed nine months. His visit was probably sometime between 679 and 688. What he saw at the Church of the Holy Sepulchre was essentially the Constantinian church restored by Modestus earlier in the century. Tradition has it that when Arculf left the Holy Land he traveled home by boat. Being sent off track by a storm he landed on the island of Iona, Scotland where he met Adomnan, abbot of the monastery there. Arculf dictated what he had seen in Jerusalem and also drew plans of the Church of the

Stone of Anointing

Holy Sepulchre on wax for the abbot. Adomnan later published an account of Arculf's journey in a work called *On the Holy Places*, which gives an account of what Arculf had seen in Jerusalem.

He had apparently seen a round church built over the tomb of Christ. This had three concentric walls and twelve columns. There were three apses containing three altars, one in each. Arculf also saw a church dedicated to Mary to the southeast; a church over the site of Golgotha; a church containing the cup which had been used at the Last Supper and in which the sponge that had been put to Jesus' mouth on the cross was kept; and still further east, the Martyrion, Constantine's main church. From Arculf's visit it is clear that Constantine's church was still basically intact with the modifications

Contemporary pilgrim crosses at the ninth station

made by Modestus in the seventh century. This situation remained the same until the eleventh century.

The next stage in the history of the church is tragic. In 1009 the Fatimid Caliph Hakim of Egypt (known as the "mad" Caliph) ordered the complete destruction of the church. The entire building including the tomb was demolished. Barely anything remained of Constantine's church apart from a section of the Rotunda. Probably because the Caliph's mother was a Christian, he apologized and allowed the Christians to begin restoration. This was carried out with the help of the Byzantine emperor. Most historians credit Constantine IX Monomachus (1042–1055) with this although some say that it was completed earlier, during the reign of Michael IV Paphlogonian (1034–1041). In any case, a much smaller building was erected renewing the Rotunda and adding an apse facing east. Three small chapels were constructed further east off the open Triportico. Other chapels were also added on the south side of the church where a new entrance was constructed. This eleventh-century church was small in comparison with Constantine's original basilica but enabled the Christians to continue worshiping at Golgotha and the tomb.

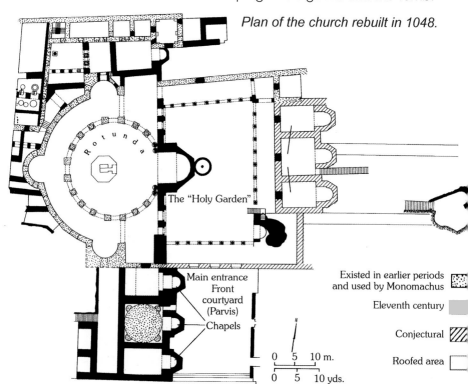

Plan of the church rebuilt in 1048.

Rotunda

The "Holy Garden"

Main entrance
Front
courtyard
(Parvis)

Chapels

Existed in earlier periods
and used by Monomachus

Eleventh century

Conjectural

Roofed area

0   5   10 m.

0   5   10 yds.

Crusader and Constantinian arches in the north aisle

THE CRUSADER CHURCH

The next period in the history of the Church of the Holy Sepulchre is that of the Crusades. After the destruction of the Constantinian church in 1009 other events in the wider region began to outrage Christians in the west. Indeed the beginning of the collapse of the great Byzantine Empire of the east began around this time. In 1071 at Manzikert in Armenia (present-day Turkey) the army of the Byzantine emperor was defeated by the Seljuk Turks. Pilgrimage to Jerusalem was affected and the Byzantine Emperor Alexius I appealed to Pope Urban II of Rome for help. At Clermont in France in 1095 Pope Urban gave a speech calling for a Crusade to recover the Christian east and the holy places of Palestine. Thus began the First Crusade. There were to be several waves of western crusading resulting in the tragic slaughtering of many Jews, Christians, and Muslims on the way. Godfrey de Bouillon led the First Crusade from France and in 1099 the Crusaders took Jerusalem and established their Latin Kingdom. Baldwin I was crowned King of Jerusalem on Christmas Day 1100 in the Church of the Nativity in Bethlehem.

It was now time for the Crusaders to turn their hands to rebuilding the Church of the Holy Sepulchre. They were in no hurry, however, as the restored building was still in good condition and they wanted to preserve their inheritance. In 1114 the Crusaders installed a community of Augustinian Canons to look after the church. They needed accommodation and space. Once again, there were also the needs of a growing pilgrimage population. Gradually the Crusaders set about redesigning the site. The church they built was finished sometime between 1149 and 1167 and was essentially the church as it is today, although many of the secondary buildings have now disappeared.

The Crusaders did a number of things. Their vision was that in Jerusalem they would surpass their best buildings in Europe. As the *edicule* and the Rotunda were in good condition the Crusaders

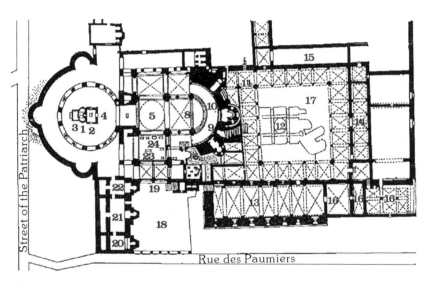

Plan of the Basilica of the Holy Sepulchre and Priory of the Canons Regular of the Holy Sepulchre, after Frs Vincent and Abel. The Crusader church was oriented in the opposite direction to that of Constantine.

1:-The Holy Sepulchre; 2:-Chapel of the Angel; 3:-Altar; 4:-Rotunda; 5:-Dome; 6:-Golgotha; 7:-Chapel of the Raising of the Cross; 8:-Choir of the Augustinian Canons; 9:-Stairs to the Crypt of St. Helena; 10:-Stairs to the Augustinian Cloister; 11:-Entrance to the Cloisters; 12:-Dome of the Crypt of St. Helena; 13:-Refectory; 14:-Chapter Room; 15:-Dormitory; 16:-Kitchen, office, stores; 17:-Cloister quadrangle; 18:-Southern Atrium; 19:-Main entrance to the Basilica; 20:-Chapel of St. James; 21:-Chapel of St. John, former Baptistery; 22:-Chapel of the Forty Martyrs; 23:-Stone of Unction; 24:-Royal Tombs.

began to develop a new church in an easterly direction, away from the tomb. The *edicule* was later richly decorated. They demolished the eastern apse from the restoration and built a vast nave and their own apse (still there today) much further east in which a high altar faced eastward. Over this area they erected a second, smaller dome, which is still there today. Three further chapels also oriented eastwards were situated in an ambulatory behind the high altar. The result was effectively a late Romanesque French cathedral that changed the entire ethos of the building and reoriented the worship eastward. The main focal points were still Calvary and the tomb, but otherwise the church was completely turned around. Also, for the first time in the church's history the various focal points (Calvary, the tomb, the Chapel of St. Helena, and the new nave and high altar) were all brought under one roof. Beyond the church, still toward the east, steps led to the domestic buildings of the Augustinian Priory. These included a refectory, chapter room, dormitory, kitchen, and office stores, all situated round a large four-sided cloister. A five-storey bell tower was added on the south in 1170. This subsequently lost several of its storeys, but the base survives today. The main entrance to the Crusader church was a double door with decorated lintels consisting of stone reliefs depicting, among other things, the Raising of Lazarus, the Entry into Jerusalem, and the Last Supper. It was a grand entrance to an impressive Crusader cathedral.

Crusader remains on the façade of the church

Crusader mosaic of the Ascension of Jesus on Latin Calvary

The Crusader Kingdom of Jerusalem lasted until July 4th, 1187 when it was defeated by the Muslim leader Saladin at the famous battle at the Horns of Hattin in Galilee. Although the Crusaders retook Jerusalem for ten years between 1229 and 1239, and continued in Akko until 1291, their kingdom was now essentially over. The victorious Saladin closed the doors of the Church of the Holy Sepulchre for three days until deciding that it was to remain in Christian hands. He closed one of the doors permanently by bricking it up. But he did not destroy the church, which has survived until today in its basic Crusader form.

Crusader doorways

Christian Groups in the Church

There are six different Christian denominations that use the Church of the Holy Sepulchre today, three major and three minor (that is, in terms of space, rights and authority within the building). The three major groups are:

(1) Greek Orthodox

The Greek Orthodox Church is the dominant Church in the Holy Land today in terms of political power and land ownership, although it is not the biggest in terms of numbers. (The largest numerically is the Melkite or Greek Catholic Church, which does not have space in the Church of the Holy Sepulchre.) The Greeks at the Church of the Holy Sepulchre are under the jurisdiction of the Greek Patriarch of Jerusalem who is under the Patriarch of Constantinople in today's Istanbul. During the Crusader period the Greek Patriarch was exiled to Constantinople. The patriarchate was restored when the Latin kingdom ended in the twelfth century. When Constantine the Great made Constantinople his capital city in the fourth century,

Greek Orthodox Catholicon or main sanctuary

the eastern part of the empire spoke Greek. Thus, today not all "Greek" Christians in the Holy Land are ethnically Greek. Many local Palestinian Arab Christians are Greek Orthodox. The Church of St. James off the Parvis near the main entrance to the church is the local parish church of the Arab Orthodox community. The Orthodox also worship in the main part of the Church of the Holy Sepulchre. The services are those of the Greek tradition and come from St. John Chrysostom (ca. 347–407) and St. Basil the Great (ca. 330–379) among others. The Greek clergy are easily recognizable by their beards and cylindrical hats.

(2) Armenian Orthodox

Armenia was the first nation to accept Christianity as its official religion in 301, some years before it became legal in the Roman Empire. Armenian Christians have been in the Holy Land since the fourth century. They arrived as pilgrims and monks and established monasteries and other institutions that have survived to the present day. They have a distinctive national presence. Their monastic

Armenian altar in St. Helen's Chapel

Catholic Franciscan Altar of St. Mary Magdalene

clergy wear black robes with a pointed hat. Like the Greeks they have a patriarch in Jerusalem. He resides in the complex of buildings at the Cathedral of St. James in the Armenian Quarter of the Old City. The Armenians are one of the non-Chalcedonian churches. They were not present at the Council of Chalcedon (in present-day Turkey) in 451 CE and did not agree with its pronouncement about the person of Jesus Christ. They are sometimes known to outsiders as "monophysites" because they claimed that when God became incarnate in Jesus there was only "one nature" (Greek: *mono*–one; *physis*–nature) after the union of the two. They have strong musical and liturgical traditions and have many institutions and schools in Jerusalem. In the Church of the Holy Sepulchre they have a chapel downstairs at the back of the main Greek sanctuary and a larger gallery upstairs near the tomb.

(3) Roman Catholic or Latin, and Franciscan

The Roman Catholics in the Holy Land are known as the "Latins." When Constantine made Constantinople his new capital in the fourth century he called it the "new Rome" and those who lived in Constantinople were called "Romans." The Greek East split from the Latin West in 1054 and when the Crusaders set up a Latin

Patriarchate in Jerusalem during the twelfth century the Catholics became known as "Latins" because they were from the Latin West. The Greeks in the Holy Land were already known as "Romans" so the Roman Catholics became known as Latins to distinguish them. When the Crusader Kingdom came to an end in 1187, the Latin patriarch was exiled and only returned to Jerusalem in 1847. Today the Latin patriarch resides at the Patriarchate in the Old City of Jerusalem just inside the New Gate. The Latins are under the Pope in Rome and use the services of the Roman Catholic Church.

In the Church of the Holy Sepulchre the Latins are Franciscan monks. They have been in charge of many of the Holy Places in the Holy Land since 1342 when they became the 'Custodians of the Holy Places'. They have played a big part in the history of this church and are recognisable by their distinctive brown habit.

They use an area of the church close to the tomb on the northern side where they have a chapel. They also have an organ (built by the Austrian organ builder Rieger), which provides a musical dimension unknown in the other traditions in this church. In general the Latin clergy dress in the catholic clerical style more familiar to westerners.

Mosaic of the Sacrifice of Isaac on Latin Calvary

The three minor groups are:

(4) Coptic Orthodox

The Coptic Orthodox Church is the Egyptian Church. The word "Copt" comes from the Greek *Aigyptos* meaning Egypt. Like the Armenians, the Copts have been in Jerusalem since the early Byzantine period

Coptic chapel at the back of the tomb of Christ

when they arrived as monks and pilgrims. Also, like the Armenians they are "non-Chalcedonian" or "monophysite." The history of the church in Egypt is long and fascinating. Antony of Egypt (251–356) was the founder of Egyptian monasticism in the third and fourth centuries; and Athanasius (ca. 296–373) and Cyril (died ca. 444), two of the great early Christian theologians, were Bishops of Alexandria. There are about fifteen million Coptic Christians in Egypt today under the Coptic Pope Tawadros II but they are a very much smaller community in Jerusalem with only a few hundred. The Copts have a little chapel at the back of the tomb inside the Church of the Holy Sepulchre. The Coptic patriarchate in Jerusalem was established in 1236 and is situated on the roof of the Church of the Holy Sepulchre where they also have the Church of St. Helena. Coptic monastic priests are distinguishable by the thin "baby's bonnet" hat they wear symbolizing "becoming like little children" (Matt 18:1–4). It is usually

black or white with twelve embroidered crosses signifying the twelve apostles. There is no Coptic patriarch today; an archbishop is in charge. The liturgy is in Coptic (the language of Christian Egypt until the tenth century) and Arabic.

Coptic chapel

Part of the Ethiopian monastery on the roof of the contemporary church.

(5) Ethiopian Orthodox

The Ethiopian Orthodox Church in Jerusalem is smaller in number than the Coptic Church. It has a fascinating relationship with Jerusalem which it claims goes back to King Solomon and the Queen of Sheba (1 Kings 10:1–13). Ethiopian tradition says that after Sheba's visit to Solomon, the couple married and gave birth to a son who became King Menelik I of Ethiopia. The bond between Israel and Ethiopia continues today and Ethiopian Christians keep the Sabbath, circumcise their male children, and take the Hebrew Bible seriously. The story of Philip and the Ethiopian (Acts 8:26–40) is also important in Ethiopian identity. Until 1952 when it became independent, the Ethiopian Church was a sister church of the Coptic Church. Like the Armenians and Copts the Ethiopians are "non-Chalcedonian" or "monophysite." The Ethiopian priests are recognizable by their small black hats (which are lower than the Greeks). Their modern, everyday language is Amharic but their liturgical language is Ge'ez, the classical language of Ethiopia. In the seventeenth century the Ethiopians were exiled by the other communities to the roof of the Church of the Holy Sepulchre where their monastery of Deir es-Sultan can still be seen today.

Ethiopian Monastery of Deir es-Sultan on the roof of the church

(6) Syrian Orthodox

The Syrian Orthodox Church has a very small place in the Church of the Holy Sepulchre today: it rents a chapel from the Armenians in the Rotunda just behind the tomb of Christ. The history of the Syrian Church is rich and complex. Like the Armenians, Copts, and Ethiopians, the Syrians are "non-Chalcedonian" or "monophysite." They are also known as the "Jacobites" after Jacob Baradaeus (ca. 500–578), an important bishop who spread the monophysite faith in Syria. Their clergy wear a distinctive circular hat similar to the

Syrian altar

Greeks. Their services are in Aramaic, the language of Jesus. Syrian Christians in Jerusalem are often to be heard playing the bagpipes. Their chief bishop in Jerusalem resides at the Syrian Church of St. Mark in the Old City, one of the possible sites of the Last Supper.

These six Christian groups all worship regularly in the Church of the Holy Sepulchre and have rights in the building under the Status Quo or agreement of 1852.

PART TWO:

GUIDE TO THE CHURCH
OF THE HOLY SEPULCHRE

APPROACHING THE CHURCH

The Church of the Holy Sepulchre is situated inside the walled Old City of Jerusalem. The nearest city gates are Damascus Gate, New Gate, and Jaffa Gate. You will find the church located at the heart of the Christian Quarter near the Lutheran Church of the Redeemer and the Muristan shopping area. An arch bearing the words "Holy Sepulchre" marks the main entrance to the Parvis or square upon which the church stands. "Parvis" means "paradise" and refers to

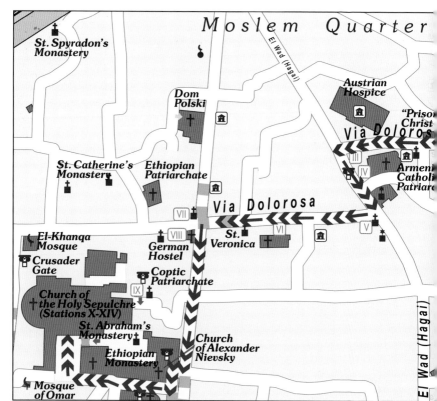

The Via Dolorosa & The Stations of the Cross

Sign over the arch leading to the Parvis

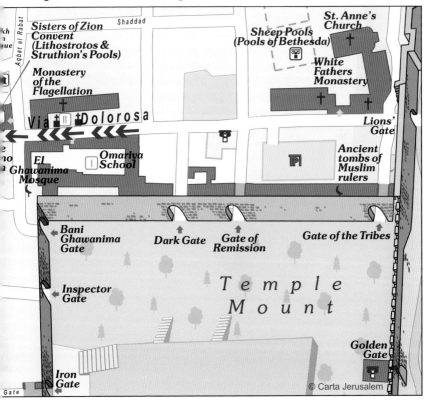

the entrance area in front of the church. Pass through the arch into the Parvis and you will immediately see the main doorway into the church.

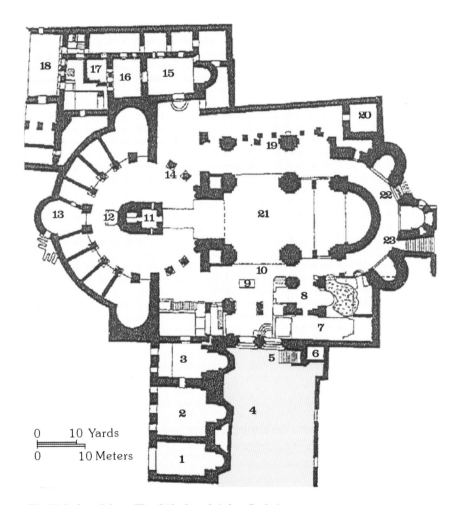

The Holy Sepulchre: The C12 church (after Corbo).

1–3. C11 chapels
4. Courtyard
5. Steps
6. Chapel of the Franks
7. Latin Calvary
8. Greek Calvary (above)
   Chapel of Adam (below)
9. Stone of Anointing
10. Greek wall

11. Tomb of Christ
12. Coptic Chapel
13. 1C tomb
14. Tapering columns
15. Chapel of St. Mary
   Magdalene
16. Franciscan choir
17. C11 atrium
18. C7 room

19. Byzantine and Crusader
   columns and piers
20. Prison of Christ
21. Greek Orthodox Catholicon
22. Entrance to medieval
   monastery
23. Entrance to Crypt of St.
   Helena.

Pillars on the left of the main door   *One of the main doors*

OUTSIDE THE CHURCH

Looking straight at the church from the Parvis you will see the great Crusader façade. On your left behind the walls are three Greek Orthodox chapels built in the eleventh century: (**1**) the Church of St. James or Mar Yacoub. This is the parish church of the local Palestinian Arab Greek Orthodox Christians. James the brother of Jesus (Mark 6:3) was the first Bishop of Jerusalem; (**2**) the Chapel of St. Mary Magdalene to whom Jesus appeared after his resurrection (Mark 16:1), sometimes known as the Chapel of St. John. The baptistery of Constantine's Basilica was originally in this area; and (**3**) the Chapel of the Forty Martyrs of Sebaste in Armenia.

On the right hand side of the Parvis behind the walls are the buildings of: (**1**) the Greek Orthodox Monastery of St. Abraham (above it out of sight are two other chapels: *(a)* of the Apostles; and *(b)* of St. Abraham); (**2**) the Armenian Chapel of St. John the Evangelist; and in the corner of the Parvis (**3**) the Coptic/Ethiopian Chapel of St. Michael the Archangel. Through the door in the corner, stairs lead up through the Chapel of St. Michael to the Ethiopian Chapel of the Four Bodiless Living Creatures and out onto the roof where the small Ethiopian monastery of Deir es-Sultan is located and remains of the Crusader refectory can be seen. The Coptic area is through an arch on the far side of the square.

Looking at the Crusader façade from the Parvis you will see to the right just outside the main door of the Church some steps leading up to the Chapel of Our Lady of Sorrows or of the Franks. Until the twelfth century this was an entrance to Calvary. Underneath this chapel behind a door is the Chapel of St. Mary of Egypt (probably fifth century) who is said to have been converted at the Church. These chapels are usually closed to the public. Until the earthquake of 1927 the two main doors of the Church had stone reliefs above them depicting scenes from the gospels including the Raising of Lazarus, Jesus' Triumphal Entry into Jerusalem, and the Last Supper. These are now in the Rockefeller Museum in East Jerusalem. The right-hand door was walled up by the Muslim leader Saladin when he took Jerusalem in 1187. Notice the famous ladder above this door. It cannot be removed because of the Status Quo agreement of 1852. In front of the doors to the right on the floor under a wooden cover is the tomb of the Crusader knight Philip d'Aubigny.

Holy Sepulchre door, hasp and knocker

Crusader arches on the façade, showing the ladder

Above the church to the left you can see the bell tower. Originally two and half storeys taller, it was built between 1160–1180 by the Crusader architect Maître Jourdain. Due to threat of collapse it was shortened in the fourteenth century and again in 1719 when the red brick roof was added.

INSIDE THE CHURCH

Pass through the main entrance of the church noticing the crack in the pillar on your left. This is connected by pilgrims with the earthquake said to have taken place at the time of Jesus' death and resurrection (Matt 27:51; 28:2). Many leave prayers on pieces of paper in the crack as they do at the Western (or "Wailing") Wall. Inside the church on your left is a bench used by representatives of the two Muslim families that keep the key to the door of the church: the Nusseibeh and Judah families. They have had possession of the key since the time of Saladin. A ceremonial unlocking takes place every day in the early morning and a locking in the evening.

Entering the church you will see a large mosaic on the wall straight ahead of you. It depicts the body of Christ being taken down from the cross (the deposition) and dates from 1991. The wall was put in by the Greeks when the church was renovated in 1810 and separates the Greek part, the Catholicon, from the rest of the building.

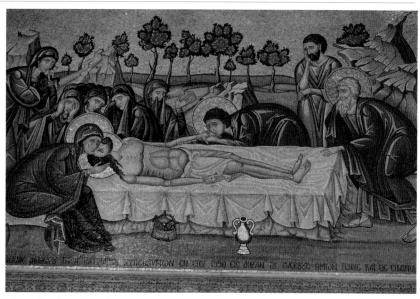

Mosaic showing the deposition of Christ from the cross

Stone of Anointing

Below the mosaic on the floor is the "Stone of Anointing" decorated with eight lamps. Also commemorating the deposition, it too dates from 1810. The stone is a focus of devotion for pilgrims who kiss it, leaving their scents and flowers. The Crusader kings Baldwin I and Baldwin II were originally buried in this part of the church along with Godfrey de Bouillon, but their bodies were removed by the Greeks in the nineteenth-century renovation.

CALVARY

Turn immediately to your right up a steep staircase and you will be on Calvary or Golgotha (Latin: *Calvaria*; Aramaic: *Golgotha,* both meaning "the place of a skull," Mark 15:22). This marks the place of Jesus' crucifixion and along with the tomb is one of the two main focal points of the church. Calvary stands on bedrock and was part of the open air courtyard in Constantine's church. It was brought inside the church when a roof was put over it at the time of the eleventh-century restoration. Four of the fourteen Stations of the Cross are commemorated on Calvary. The first nine are along the Via Dolorosa in the Old City of Jerusalem. The fourteenth is the tomb. Station ten is remembered at the top of the stairs up to Calvary. When you get to the top you will see two main chapels, the

Stairs up to Calvary

Roman Catholic, Latin or Franciscan chapel on the right and the Greek Orthodox chapel on the left.

The Latin chapel marks the eleventh station. Notice the mosaic behind the altar, depicting Christ being nailed to the cross. Also notice a portrayal of the Binding of Isaac (Gen 22:1–19) in the mosaic on the wall to the right above the window. Christians see this story as a foreshadowing of the sacrifice of Jesus on the cross. Another mosaic on the wall depicts Jesus meeting the women of Jerusalem (Luke 23:27–31). Mosaics also adorn the ceiling and include images of four Old Testament prophets, Saints Peter and Paul, and other images. The only remaining Crusader mosaic is that of the Ascension of Christ in the center of the ceiling. The entire area was restored by the Italian architect Antonio Barluzzi in 1937.

On the left-hand side of Calvary is the Greek Orthodox altar with a huge crucifix marking the spot believed to be the place of Jesus' crucifixion. Images of the mother of Jesus and the Beloved Disciple (John 19:25–27) can also be seen. This altar marks the twelfth station. Underneath is a hole through which you may put your hand to touch the rock of Calvary, which can be seen surrounding the area and under glass. Notice the crack in the bedrock to the right of this altar. Again, pilgrims associate this with the earthquake at the

Calvary: Greek chapel

Calvary: Latin or Roman Catholic chapel

time of Jesus' death (Matt 27:51). The crack can also be seen in the bedrock visible in the Chapel of Adam below Calvary. The ceiling of the Greek part of Calvary is decorated with various paintings depicting scenes from the passion of Christ. Notice the small Greek altar on the left of the main altar and the pulpit with images of the four evangelists.

Between the main Greek and Latin altars on Calvary stands the Altar of our Lady of Sorrows, also Latin. This marks the thirteenth station. In a glass case on the altar is a statue of Mary with a sword piercing her heart. The statue was given by Queen Maria 1 Braganza of Portugal and was brought from Lisbon in 1778. The sword symbolises the pain that Mary underwent at the death of her son (Luke 2:35).

Chapel of Adam underneath Calvary

THE ROTUNDA AND TOMB

Leave Calvary by the steps opposite the ones you ascended. At the bottom turn left crossing the area of the Stone of Anointing. You will soon come to the Armenian area of the church. On your left is the freestanding Place of the Three Marys commemorating their presence at the cross at the time of the crucifixion (John 19:25). Also notice the huge mosaic of the crucifixion (1970) on the wall and the Armenian sacristy to the left. There is also a staircase here leading up to the Armenian Gallery where there are further altars

Armenian mosaic of Noah's Ark

and mosaics. This is usually closed to the public although permission to enter is sometimes given by the Armenians. It is worth asking.

Continue round to the right and you will soon see the contemporary tomb of Christ straight ahead of you. The gospel of John tells us that 'there was a garden in the place where he was crucified, and in the garden there was a new tomb' (19:41) where they laid Jesus. The close proximity of Calvary and the tomb is striking. The contemporary tomb is in the Rotunda or domed part of the church. It stands at the center of the Rotunda surrounded by pillars. Some of these may date back to the church of Constantine. In that church this area was next to the open-air Triportico. A cover was added soon after Constantine's reign but the entire area was only covered during the eleventh-century restoration. The contemporary tomb of Christ or *edicule* (Latin: "little house") dates from the nineteenth century. It may well stand over the site of Christ's actual tomb, but this was destroyed completely by the Caliph Hakim in 1009 if not before. Walk around the tomb noting the holes in the walls. The "new fire" is passed through these holes on Orthodox Easter Saturday at the service of "Holy Fire," a ceremony dating back at least to the ninth century.

At the back of the tomb is a small Coptic chapel dedicated to the Holy Virgin. Originally dating from the sixteenth century, it was restored in the nineteenth. The chapel is said to mark the spot where Christ's head was placed in burial and a stone underneath the altar

Chapel of the Angel inside the tomb of Christ

Main shelf inside the tomb of Christ

is said to be part of the original tomb. Pilgrims are invited to reach under the altar to touch the original stone. The Copts are one of the smaller Oriental Orthodox groups that use the church.

Opposite the Coptic chapel there is a doorway into the Syrian Orthodox Chapel of St. Nicodemus. Enter and you will soon notice that it is in very bad condition. This is a symptom of the infamous bad relations between the various groups of Christians who use the Church. In this case the problem concerns the Syrians and the Armenians. The chapel is owned by the Armenians but is leased to the Syrians. The Armenians will not renovate the chapel because they do not use it. The Syrians will not renovate it because they do not own it. The chapel remains in bad condition although a new floor has now been laid. Just off this chapel opposite the doorway is a small cave area containing two *kochim* (or "rolling stone") tombs in fairly good condition. These are called the tombs of Joseph of Arimathea and of Nicodemus recalling the characters in the gospels that assisted in Jesus' burial (John 19:38–42). The burial procedure described in the Introduction to this Guide fits perfectly here. This was a rolling stone tomb with niches for at least two bodies. The rolling stone itself has now disappeared. These two tombs are certainly closer in style to the one in which Jesus was likely to have been buried than is the large nineteenth-century tomb in the Rotunda. They also indicate that this area was outside the city wall at the time of Jesus' death and burial thus adding weight to the argument that this site is authentic. Leave the Syrian chapel and turn left. Walk around the large tomb of Christ and turn right to its main entrance.

The contemporary tomb structure dates from 1810 and along with Calvary is one of the two main focal points of Christian devotion in the church today. Constantine's *edicule* was destroyed in the eleventh century and was restored many times, for example by the Franciscan Boniface of Ragusa in 1555. It was restored most recently in 1829 and is held together by steel bands put on during the period of the British Mandate (1917–1947). At the front of the structure you can see two low walls upon which are candles belonging to the Greeks and the Armenians.

Now enter the contemporary tomb of Christ. Today, it is divided into two parts. Walk into the first part. This is the Chapel of the Angel

Inside the dome over the Greek Catholicon

Pilgrim crosses from the Crusader period

and commemorates the angel that appeared when the women went to the tomb and found the stone rolled away (Matt 28:2). A piece of stone reputed to be part of the rolling stone of Jesus' tomb is preserved in a small stone container at the center of this chapel and is used as an altar by the Greeks.

Walk through to the main part of the tomb and you will see a shelf that forms the main focus of the tomb. Today, the interior of this tomb bears no resemblance to a *koch* tomb of the time of Jesus. Above the tomb shelf are three images of the Resurrection of Christ belonging to the three main communities in the church: Greek, Armenian, and Latin. The words *Christos Aneste* in Greek mean "Christ is Risen." Although the floor space of this tomb may be where Jesus' tomb was, nothing now remains of his actual tomb.

Leave the tomb and walk straight ahead. You can now see into the main body of the Greek Orthodox Catholikon or sanctuary. From this position you will be able to see that the building is largely a French Cathedral in the Romanesque-Gothic style. Look ahead and you will see two thrones: on the left is that of the Patriarch of Antioch, and on the right that of the Patriarch of Jerusalem. Look up and see some of the many modern mosaics added in 1991. Here are apostles, evangelists, and fathers of the church.

Now turn around and, facing the tomb, look up and see the inside of the Rotunda above the tomb. This is decorated with twelve golden bands symbolizing the twelve apostles. Each has three points symbolizing the Trinity. The background is decorated with gold stars and was completed in 1996 and dedicated in 1997 after many years of negotiation and planning.

Walk to your right and you will see the Roman Catholic, Latin or Franciscan section of the church. The first altar on the right is that of St. Mary Magdalene, commemorating the appearance of the risen Christ to Mary when she thought he was the gardener (John 20:11–18). Straight ahead you will pass through a door into a separate

chapel. This is the main Latin Chapel of the Apparition of Jesus to his Mother. The two bronze doors, given in 1982, are from Australia. Notice the Stations of the Cross on the far wall of the chapel and the Column of the Flagellation upon which it is said Christ was whipped (Matt 27:26). The Blessed Sacrament is reserved in this chapel. In the sacristy are spurs and a sword said to be those of the Crusader Godfrey de Bouillon.

Looking up at the inside of the Rotunda
Photo: Samuel Magal

Franciscan Chapel of the Apparition of Jesus to his Mother

CHAPELS AROUND THE CHURCH

Leave the Latin chapel and turn left into the north aisle of the church. Stand in the center and look up at the arches. It is possible

Crusader and Constantinian arches in the north aisle

to discern arches and capitals from both the Crusader and the Constantinian churches here. In the left-hand corner of the north aisle at the opposite end you will find the Chapel of the Prison of Christ. A ninth-century tradition states that Jesus was kept here with the two thieves before his crucifixion (cf. Luke 23:32–33).

Greek Chapel of the Crowning with Thorns

Continue to follow the aisle around and you will soon come to two chapels on the left. The first is the Greek Chapel of St. Longinus, recalling the soldier who pierced Jesus' side with a spear (John 19:34). The Greek word for "spear" (*longche*) gave the soldier his name in later Christian tradition. The second is the Armenian Chapel of the Division of the Raiment, commemorating the dividing of Jesus' clothes (John 19:23–24).

Greek Chapel of St. Longinus

Armenian Chapel of the Division of the Raiment

The main wall opposite these altars is the outside of the apse of the Greek Orthodox Catholicon. It is important to pause here for a moment. As was noted in the Introduction to this Guide, the original church built by Constantine was oriented in the opposite direction compared to the contemporary church. If you look at the outside of the wall of the apse you will be looking west in the direction of the tomb. Constantine's high altar would have been in this region. However, when the church was rebuilt in the eleventh and twelfth centuries, the orientation was changed and the high altar now faced east. The Crusaders left it this way and so it remains today. The main Greek high altar area is behind this apse.

Next you will come to a staircase on the left. This leads down first to the Armenian Chapel of St. Helena and then to the Chapel of the Finding of the Holy Cross. On your way down notice the many Crusader pilgrim crosses carved in the stone on the right- and left-hand walls.

When you reach the bottom of the twenty-nine steps you will be standing in the Armenian Chapel of St. Helena. The Armenians are one of the six Christian groups that use the church. The Armenian altar is easily recognizable from the series of steps at the back of the altar. These symbolize the ascent of the soul to heaven and are common in Armenian churches. This step symbolism was used in ancient Zoroastrian altars and found its way into Armenian Christianity. The specifically Armenian flavor of the chapel is found in the beautiful mosaic floor. In the center is a depiction of the capital city of Etchmiadzin in Armenia where the Catholicos, or chief bishop, of the Armenian Orthodox Church resides. Other parts of the mosaic depict Noah's Ark on Mount Ararat (now in Turkey). Around the walls of this chapel are paintings depicting historic events in the history of Christianity in Armenia.

Behind a door on the left-hand side of this chapel, stairs lead down to the Armenian excavations and the Chapel of St. Vartan. These are usually closed to the public but permission to visit is sometimes given by the Armenian authorities. The excavations, carried out in the 1970s, uncovered an inscription of a boat with the words *domine ivimus* meaning "Lord we came" or "Lord we arrived." The inscription is difficult to date and has been interpreted in different ways. It is said by some to have been etched by a fourth-century pilgrim who had traveled to Jerusalem by boat across the Mediterranean Sea. Parts of the foundations of Constantine's basilica can also be seen

Under the altar on Greek Calvary

in this area. It is worth asking an Armenian priest for permission to go down.

On the south side of the Armenian Chapel to your right as you face the altar is more of the bedrock that continues down to the next chapel below. Take the twenty-two steps down and you will be in the Chapel of the Finding of the Cross, sometimes called the Chapel of the Invention of the Cross. Above the altar you will see a modern statue of St. Helen holding the cross. This was a gift of Archduke Maximilian of Austria. Ambrose of Milan (ca. 339–397) says that Helen discovered the "true cross" when the tomb of Jesus was being dug up in the fourth century. Rufinus (ca. 345–410) adds that three crosses were discovered in a nearby cistern and were laid upon sick people. The one that healed them was deemed to be the cross of Christ. Frescoes from the Crusader period have recently been restored in this chapel and can be seen behind glass on your right.

Now make your way back up the steps into the Armenian Chapel and up the second flight of steps back into the main part of the church.

Turn left at the top of the stairs and you will see on your left the

Candles burning near the tomb of Christ

Greek Chapel of the Crowning with Thorns (also known as the Chapel of the Derision or Mocking). This commemorates the mocking of Jesus by the soldiers during his trial (Matt 27:27–31). Under the altar is displayed part of a pillar that Jesus is said to have sat upon during this mocking. Continue in the same direction and you will see on your left a huge piece of rock displayed behind glass. This is more bedrock, which continues down from Calvary above you.

Continue straight and (again on your left) enter the Chapel of Adam, which lies directly underneath Calvary. The chapel connects Christ with Adam and reflects a development in early Christian thinking that saw an important relation between the two. St. Paul, for example, calls Jesus the "last Adam" and the "second man" (1 Cor 15:45–47; cf. Rom 5:12–21). Before long, the early Christians thought of Adam as having died in the region of Christ's death. Both Origen of Alexandria (ca. 185–ca. 254) and Epiphanius of Salamis (ca. 315–403) mention this. Epiphanius says that when Jesus died, his blood wetted Adam's skull. Notice the crack in the rock behind the glass above the altar in this chapel. It is said by some to have been caused by the earthquake at the time of Jesus' death (Matt 27:51).

AND FINALLY...

...leave the Chapel of Adam and turn left. You will see the Stone of Anointing and the modern mosaic of the Deposition of Jesus from the Cross on the wall above it. Turn left past the stone and you will see the main entrance where you came in. Leave by this door and you will find yourself back in the Parvis where you began. The exit back into the main street is in the far left-hand corner of the Parvis.

CHURCH OF THE HOLY SEPULCHRE: A ROUGH CHRONOLOGY

BCE .... Area outside the city wall is a quarry.

30–33 CE... Jesus of Nazareth crucified in the quarry outside the city wall of Jerusalem.

41–44........ Jerusalem city wall extended (the third wall) by Herod Agrippa. Place of crucifixion now falls inside the walls.

70............... Jerusalem falls to the Romans.

135 .... Emperor Hadrian builds a Temple to Aphrodite/Venus over the area.

335............ 14th September, Constantine's Basilica dedicated.

381–384..... Egeria visits Jerusalem.

614............. Persians attack Jerusalem. Church badly damaged inside.

629............. Church renovated under Abbot Modestus.

638............. Muslims attack Jerusalem. Patriarch Sophronius surrenders to the Caliph Omar. Church survives.

679–688..... Arculf visits the Holy Land and describes the church to Adomnan.

1009.......... Church largely destroyed by the "mad" Egyptian Caliph Hakim.

1034–55..... Church rebuilt under either Michael IV Paphlogonian (1034–1041) or Constantine IX Monomachus (1042–1055) and reoriented in an easterly direction.

1099.......... First Crusade arrives in Jerusalem under Godfrey de Bouillon. Latin Kingdom of Jerusalem established.

1114.......... Crusaders install a community of Augustinian Canons.

1149–1167. Crusaders rebuild the church.

1187.......... 4th July, Crusaders defeated by Saladin at the Horns of Hattin. Jerusalem retaken by Muslims. Crusader building remains.

1187–1517. Muslim rule.

1517–1917 Ottoman rule.

1555.......... Edicule rebuilt by Boniface of Ragusa.

1808.......... Fire causes damage in the church.

1810.......... Parts of the church renovated.

1852.......... The Status Quo - an agreement about the rights of the several communities in the church.

1917–1947 British rule.

1927.......... Earthquake shakes the church.

1934.......... Another fire damages the church.

1948–1967 Jordanian rule.

1949.......... Another fire damages the church.

1950.......... Agreement to undertake repairs on the church.

1967.......... Israel occupies East Jerusalem including the Old City.

1997.......... Restoration of Rotunda completed.

1. Entrance to Holy Sepulchre Church
2. The stone of anointing
3. Chapel of Adam (Greek)
4. Mount Calvary
5. Chapel of Greek Orthodox
6. Greek enclosure wall
7. Justinian's Apse (Greek)
8. Continuation of the rock of Calvary
9. St. Helena's Chapel (Armenian)
10. Grotto of the Cross (Latin)
11. Statue of St. Helena (Latin)
12. Matyrium of Armenians

13 Roof of St. Helena's Chapel
14 9th Station
15 Prison of Christ (Traditional) Greek
16 The Latin Gallery
17 Chapel of Mary Magdelene (Latin)
18 Great Dome of the Holy Sepulchre
19 Tomb of Christ (All Rites)

20 Ancient clock-tower (Greek)
21 Where Holy Women viewed the Crucifixion (Armenian)
22 Entrance to Greek Patriarchate
23 Courtyard of Greek Patriarchate
24 Greek Chapel of Mary Magdelene
25 Chapel of St. James

Lamps inside the tomb of Christ

BIBLIOGRAPHY AND FURTHER READING

A. On the Gospel Passion and Resurrection Narratives

Borg, Marcus J., and John Dominic Crossan. *The Last Week: What the Gospels Really Teach About Jesus's Final Days in Jerusalem.* New York: HarperOne, 2006.

Bovon, François. *The Last Days of Jesus.* Louisville: Westminster John Knox, 2006.

Brown, Raymond. *The Death of the Messiah: From Gethsemane to the Grave; A Commentary on the Passion Narratives in the Four Gospels.* Anchor Bible Reference Library. New York: Doubleday, 1994.

Dewsnap Meinhardt, Molly, ed. *Jesus: The Last Day; A Collection of Essays Published by the Biblical Archaeology Society.* Washington, DC: Biblical Archaeology Society, 2003.

Evans, Craig A. *Jesus and the Ossuaries*. Waco, TX: Baylor University Press, 2003.

Evans, Craig A., N. T. Wright, and Troy A. Miller. *Jesus, the Final Days: What Really Happened*. London: SPCK, 2008.

Gooder, Paula. *Journey to the Empty Tomb*. Norwich: Canterbury Press, 2014.

Hengel, Martin. *Crucifixion in the Ancient World and the Folly of the Message of the Cross*. London: SCM, 1977.

Houlden, Leslie. *Backward into Light: The Passion and Resurrection of Jesus according to Matthew and Mark*. London: SCM, 1987.

Ramsey, Michael. *The Narratives of the Passion*. London: Mowbray, 1962.

Rivkin, Ellis. *What Crucified Jesus?* London: SCM, 1984.

Sloyan, Gerard S. *The Crucifixion of Jesus: History, Myth, Faith*. Minneapolis: Fortress, 1995.

Vermes, Geza. *The Passion*. London: Penguin, 2005.

Vermes, Geza. *The Resurrection*. London: Penguin, 2008.

Wansbrough, Henry. *The Passion and Death of Jesus*. London: Darton Longman & Todd, 2003.

B. On Jerusalem and the Church of the Holy Sepulchre

Bahat, Dan. *Carta's Historical Atlas of Jerusalem: An Illustrated Survey*. Jerusalem: Carta, 1986.

Biddle, Martin & Gideon Avni, Jon Seligman and Tamar Winter, *The Church of the Holy Sepulchre*. New York: Rizzoli, 2000.

Biddle, Martin. *The Tomb of Christ*. Gloucestershire: Sutton Publishing, 1999.

Cohen, Raymond. *Saving the Holy Sepulchre: How Rival Christians Came Together to Rescue Their Holiest Shrine*. Oxford: Oxford University Press, 2008.

Coüasnon, Charles. *The Church of the Holy Sepulchre in Jerusalem.* London: Oxford University Press, 1974.

Duckworth, H. T. F. *The Church of the Holy Sepulchre.* London: Hodder and Stoughton, 1922.

Duncan, Alistair. *The Noble Heritage: Jerusalem and Christianity; A Portrait of the Church of the Resurrection.* London: Longman, 1974.

Eusebius of Caesarea. *Life of Constantine.* Limovia.net.

Finegan, Jack. *The Archaeology of the New Testament: The Life of Jesus and the Beginning of the Early Church.* New Jersey: Princeton University Press, Revised Edition 1992.

Freedman, David Noel, ed. *The Anchor Bible Dictionary.* New York: Doubleday, 1992, article on 'Jerusalem' by Philip J. King, Vol 3, pp. 747-766.

Freeman-Grenville, G. S. P. *The Basilica of the Holy Sepulchre in Jerusalem.* Jerusalem: Carta, 1994.

Gibson, Shimon, and Joan E. Taylor. *Beneath the Church of the Holy Sepulchre, Jerusalem: The Archaeology and Early History of Traditional Golgotha.* London: Palestine Exploration Fund, 1994.

Harvey, William, and Ernest Tatham Richmond. *The Church of the Holy Sepulchre, Jerusalem: Structural Survey, Final Report.* London: Oxford University Press, 1935.

Hoppe, Leslie J. *The Synagogues and Churches of Ancient Palestine.* Minnesota: The Liturgical Press, 1994.

McCane, Byron R. *Roll Back the Stone: Death and Burial in the World of Jesus.* Harrisburg, PA: Trinity Press International, 2003.

Meinhardt, Jack, ed. *Crusaders in the Holy Land: The Archaeology of Faith.* Washington, DC: Biblical Archaeology Society, 2005.

Morris, Colin. *The Sepulchre of Christ and the Medieval West: From the Beginning to 1600.* Oxford: Oxford University Press, 2005.

Parrot, André. *Golgotha and the Church of the Holy Sepulchre.* London: SCM, 1957.

Stern, Ephraim, ed. *The New Encyclopedia of Archaeological Excavations in the Holy Land.* Jerusalem and New York: Simon and Schuster, and Carta Ltd., 1993, articles on 'Jerusalem' by various authors pp. 698-800.

Taylor, Joan E. *Christians and the Holy Places: The Myth of Jewish-Christian Origins.* Oxford: Clarendon, 1993.

Tsafrir, Yoram, ed. *Ancient Churches Revealed.* Jerusalem: Israel Exploration Society, 1993.

Walker, Peter. *Holy City, Holy Places? Christian Attitudes to Jerusalem and the Holy Land in the Fourth Century.* Oxford: Clarendon, 1990.

Wright, J. Robert. *The Holy Sepulchre: The Church of the Resurrection; An Ecumenical Guide.* Jerusalem: Ecumenical Theological Research Fraternity in Israel, 1995.

Lights within the tomb of Christ.

Altar of Our Lady of Sorrows on Calvary